AF422851

The Unofficial Guide to Surviving College:

Book 1: How Not to College

Future First, Inc.

Presents a book by:

Leslie Hayes, B.S.

And

Eugene Hayes, Ph.D., MBA

Contents

About the Authors

The father-son duo of Dr. Eugene Hayes and his son, Leslie Hayes, brings a unique blend of experience and perspective to their co-authored book, The Unofficial Guide to Surviving College. Dr. Hayes' extensive career in public health, leadership, and mentoring coupled with Leslie's recent college experience and trials and errors, make them the perfect team to guide incoming college students and parents through the challenges of college life.

Dr. Hayes has served over 22 years in public service, holding various leadership positions in healthcare administration, mental health, substance abuse prevention, and management. He has led several national programs in the public health sector and has been recognized with numerous United States Military and Public Health Uniformed Service awards for his outstanding service.

Leslie Hayes recently graduated from Saint Leo University with a bachelor's degree in healthcare administration. Throughout his college experience, he encountered various challenges that shaped his perspective on life and the importance of perseverance. Leslie's struggles and involvement inspired him to co-author this book with his father.

Together, Dr. Eugene Hayes and Leslie Hayes have written a guide; the first in a series, to help newly enrolled college students (and their parents) navigate the challenges of college life. Their expertise and insights make the book relatable, applicable, and invaluable for anyone looking to survive and thrive during their college years, and it is a great read for those looking for a good laugh.

Preface

The stories in this book reflect on some of the defining moments of my (Leslie) college life. Each chapter explores an experience that taught me a valuable lesson and transformed me into who I am today. From spending $3000 on vending machines to the consequences of indulgence to the importance of following a rubric or not engaging in the forbidden topics, each story is unique in its own way, yet they are all connected by a common thread: the power of learning from our mistakes.

As I share my stories, I hope to inspire others to reflect on their own experiences and learn from my mistakes because it is impossible to learn from others' mistakes. Long story short, we all make mistakes. What we learn from those mistakes, to how we choose to outgrow those mistakes define us. Through my own experiences, I have learned the importance of perseverance, resilience, and self-reflection, and I hope my stories can serve as a reminder that if I can learn and grow from my mistakes, so can you.

I want to dedicate this book to all the individuals who have been a part of my journey and helped shape me into who I am today. Whether it was a teacher who challenged me to do better, a friend who supported me during a tough time, or a family member who offered words of wisdom, each individual played a role in my personal and professional development.

Introduction

There are moments in our lives that shape us into the person we are today. Whether a triumph, a mistake, or a combination of both, these experiences profoundly impact our perspectives, behaviors, and growth. This book will share some of the defining moments of my life and the lessons I have learned along the way.

From the consequences of indulgence to the importance of following a rubric, each chapter explores a different experience and the lessons I have learned from it. These stories are not just about me but also about the people who have played a significant role in my transformative journey and the lessons that they have taught me.

While each chapter is unique, they are all connected by a common theme: the power of learning from our mistakes. It's easy to get caught up in our successes and forget the lessons our failures offer. But we have the greatest growth opportunities in these moments of difficulty and challenge.

Through my experiences, I have learned the importance of perseverance, resilience, and self-reflection. I hope that by sharing my stories, I can inspire others to reflect on their own experiences and embrace the power of learning from their mistakes.

Chapter 1: The Time I Blew $3,000 on Vending Machines

In my first year of college, I lived in a dorm with vending machines on every floor. These machines were stocked with snacks and drinks, including (pop) soda, energy drinks, and bottled water. As a busy student, I relied heavily on these vending machines to keep me fueled throughout the day.

I used the vending machines multiple times daily, always reaching for my favorite drinks (*Mello Yellow at $4.00 a bottle*). To stay hydrated, I always grabbed something from the vending machine, whether an ice-cold soda or a water bottle. I never thought much about the cost of these drinks until I received my credit card statement at the end of the semester. I had spent over $3,000 on vending machine drinks alone – a staggering amount.

At the time, vending machines seemed a good idea because they were convenient and easily accessible. However, looking back, I realized that I was overspending on drinks that were overpriced and not very healthy. I also started to feel guilty about the money I had wasted and missed opportunities to save and invest.

They were shocked when I called my parents and informed them about my overspending. My dad, who was a financial planner, gave me some tough love and told me that I needed to start budgeting and tracking my expenses. He suggested that I start buying my drinks at local stores instead of relying on vending machines, and I set a weekly spending limit for myself.

Overspending on vending machine drinks significantly impacted my overall financial situation. It left me with less money for other expenses, such as textbooks and transportation. Besides, I missed out on the opportunity to save or invest the money I had spent on vending machine drinks.

To make matters worse, my parents were also concerned about my spending habits. They had noticed that I was constantly running out of money and struggling to make ends meet. We had a long conversation about the importance of budgeting and saving, and they offered to help me develop a financial plan.

This experience taught me the importance of budgeting and planning for expenses. I realized that I needed to track my spending and cut back on unnecessary purchases consciously. I started bringing my water bottle and filling it up at water fountains around campus and shopping at local stores to save money on drinks. I also began to limit my consumption of soda and energy drinks, opting for healthier and cheaper options like tea and juice.

My experience of overspending on vending machine drinks taught me a valuable lesson about budgeting and saving money. By talking to my parents and seeking their advice, I got back on track and avoided making the same mistake again. I hope that by sharing this story, I can help others make more informed financial decisions and avoid the pitfalls of overspending.

Chapter 2: Learning to Follow the Rubric: The Time I Had to Retake a Class Six Times

I was excited when I enrolled in the college because I have always been fascinated by the courses one can take to enhance their intellectuality. So, during my starter year of college, I was eager to take on new challenges, including a course on scientific writing. As a creative writing major, I thought it would be an easy class. I was under the impression that I'd ace it because I was not afraid of writing. However, it turned out to be an interesting but challenging class. I quickly found myself struggling to keep up with the expectations of the course.

Despite my best efforts, I struggled to follow the rubric and produce the kind of writing the professor sought. My head was in the wrong place. I made careless mistakes, missed important details, and often went off tangents. I made basic mistakes that a fifth grader would make. I do not know what happened. All I knew was that I received a failing grade on my first assignment due to my arrogance and had to retake the course.

Over the next two years, I retook the class six times, each time thinking I had finally figured out how to write scientifically. But no matter how hard I tried; I always fell short. It was frustrating, humiliating, and exhausting.

Looking back, I realized I had been approaching the class all wrong. Instead of seeing it as an opportunity to learn and grow, I treated it as a hurdle to overcome. I had been so focused on getting a passing grade that I had neglected to understand the material and the professor's expectations truly.

The consequences of my poor academic performance were far-reaching. I had to repeat the class multiple times, which set me back in terms of graduation and cost me much more than I had initially speculated. Additionally, the experience took a toll on my mental health, leaving me feeling defeated and demoralized.

When I finally realized I needed help, I contacted my professors and peers. I started attending office hours and seeking feedback on my writing. I also utilized the resources provided by the writing center on campus. Slowly but surely, I began to see improvement in my writing and my grades.

This experience taught me the importance of understanding expectations and following the rubric. I realized that to succeed academically, I needed to approach assignments with a clear and focused mindset and truly take the time to understand the material truly. I also learned the importance of seeking help and guidance when I needed it, whether from peers, professors, or tutors.

Looking back on my experience, I wish I had approached the class more positively. Instead of seeing it as a burden, I could have seen it as an opportunity to learn and grow. Instead of attending the class with an open mindedness, I became close-minded, which hurt my learning. I thought I knew everything because I was a creative writing major. Had I thought I knew nothing and needed to learn to write scientifically, I could have passed this class with flying colors. Later, my interactions with my professors and peers during the class were helpful, and I wish I had utilized them more effectively.

My experience of retaking the scientific writing class six times over the first two years of school taught me a valuable lesson about the importance of following the rubric and understanding expectations. By sharing my story, I hope to encourage others to approach academic challenges with a growth mindset and a willingness to learn and to seek help and guidance when needed.

Chapter 3: Learning to Let Go: The Time I Tore My Labrum Trying to Block a Shot

During my third year of college, I felt like I could perform like the high school soccer star I once was. So, when my best friend asked me to play keeper in a pick-up game on a rainy day, I eagerly accepted the challenge, determined to show off my skills.

As the game progressed, my competitive spirit took over. I wanted to win at all costs because that was all I knew. I became gritty. My friend was a skilled player. However, I was getting frustrated trying to keep up with him. I forgot that I was no longer in my prime. So, when he took a shot on goal, I leaped forward to block it, ignoring the wet field conditions.

The fall was sudden and painful, and I immediately knew something was wrong. I had torn my *labrum* and knew that recovery would be a long and difficult process. The injury left me feeling irritated and defeated as I realized that my desire to prove myself resulted in severe consequences.

Now that when I recall this incident, I realize that I had been holding onto my past achievements for far too long. When I played soccer in high school, I was a goalkeeper. When I was young, I developed a sense of pride. I was quick to respond. I am much older and slower because I have not played soccer in a while. I had failed to realize that my skills had diminished over time, and I was no longer in the same physical shape that I once was.

I also realized that my competitive spirit had taken over, and I had become so focused on winning that I had neglected to take care of my body and understand my limitations. I had let my desire to impress my friend and prove myself as a great goalkeeper cloud my judgment, resulting in a severe injury.

The consequences of my actions were severe. I had to undergo surgery to repair my torn labrum, which left me in pain and discomfort for weeks. I also had to take time off from playing soccer, which was a huge blow to my ego and identity as a former athlete.

But through the experience, I learned some valuable lessons. I realized it was important to let go of past achievements and focus on the present. I also learned the importance of caring for my body and understanding my limitations. Finally, I learned that it was important to prioritize safety over competition, especially when playing sports with friends.

My experience of tearing my labrum while playing soccer taught me a valuable lesson about the importance of letting go of past achievements and prioritizing safety over the competition. By sharing my story, I hope to encourage others to care for their bodies and prioritize safety, even when engaging in competitive activities.

Chapter 4: The Freshman 20: How I Gained Weight in College

As a college freshman, I was excited to have the freedom to choose my food finally. However, I soon found myself gaining weight without even realizing it. As a busy student, I relied heavily on the campus dining hall for my meals.

The campus dining hall was the main food source for students, offering all-you-can-eat buffets for breakfast, lunch, and dinner. The food was not always of the best quality, but it was free and easily accessible. I indulged in unhealthy food choices and did not pay attention to portion sizes.

I gained 20 pounds in just one semester without even noticing it. My clothes started feeling tighter, and I felt less confident in my body. I also noticed that my health was starting to suffer, with borderline high cholesterol levels.

The experience took place on campus, primarily in the dining hall. No one was directly involved, as it was a personal struggle. However, I did have friends who were experiencing similar issues.

At first, I didn't realize the extent of the weight gain and brushed it off as just a natural part of the college experience. However, as my clothes became tight and my health started to suffer, I became increasingly upset with myself. I felt like I had let myself go and was disappointed in my lack of self-control.

Looking back, I realize that I didn't have the necessary knowledge and tools to make healthy food choices. I also prioritize my health as much as I should have. I realized that I needed to take ownership of my health and well-being.

The weight gain and health issues affected my self-esteem and confidence. I also realized I needed to change my diet and lifestyle to prevent further health problems. I felt empowered to take control of my health and make positive changes.

After recognizing the problem, I started to make healthier food choices and exercise more regularly. I also learned about the importance of portion control and balanced nutrition. I lost the weight I had gained and felt much better about my body and health.

The experience taught me the importance of caring for my body and health. It also motivated me to change my lifestyle and eating habits positively. I became more conscious of what I was putting into my body and made exercise a regular part of my routine.

It's important to be aware of our food choices and their impact on our health. Balancing nutrition and exercise is key to maintaining a healthy weight and lifestyle. We should also prioritize our health and make it a priority in our daily lives.

Plan meals ahead of time, practice portion control, and prioritize regular exercise. Seek support from friends or professionals if necessary. It's never too late to make positive changes to improve your health.

Chapter 5: Late Nights and Coffee Stains

During my junior year of college, I was given a 13-page final term paper assignment due in two weeks. I foolishly told myself that I could finish the paper in three days and did not take any steps to plan out the assignment.

As the days passed, I struggled to start the paper. After a week, I had made no progress and could only come up with a title for the paper. With only one week left, I began to panic as I realized I had no idea how to tackle the assignment.

By day 13 of the 14-day deadline, I finally accepted that I needed to start working on the paper. I went to a local 24-hour Denny's with my laptop and every intention of pulling an all-nighter to finish the paper. I drank all the coffee in the restaurant and had a 5-hour energy to keep me going.

I typed feverishly for the next 12 hours, ignoring the tiredness and discomfort. I prayed for a C+ on the paper, and when I finally submitted it, I had no idea what grade I would receive.

Looking back, I realized I had made a huge mistake by not taking the assignment seriously and not planning ahead of time. I had allowed myself to procrastinate and put the assignment off until the last minute, which caused me great stress and anxiety.

The aftermath of my procrastination was a feeling of relief at having finished the paper and the realization that I could have done much better if I had not put it off until the last minute. I received a B+ on the paper, which was better than I had expected given the circumstances, but I knew that I could have done better if I had given myself more time.

The experience taught me the importance of planning and breaking down tasks into smaller, more manageable parts. It also showed me the negative consequences of procrastination and its impact on academic performance and mental health.

To avoid the same mistake, I suggest creating a plan and breaking down assignments into smaller tasks to make them more manageable. Start working on assignments as early as possible and use resources such as tutors or professors for guidance and feedback.

My experience with procrastination and last-minute scrambling taught me the importance of planning and taking assignments seriously. Learning from my mistakes improved my academic performance and mental well-being. I hope that by sharing this story, I can encourage others to avoid procrastination and take their assignments seriously.

Chapter 6: A Night to Regret

I threw a party at my off-campus apartment during my junior year of college. I invited a bunch of people, mostly friends, and acquaintances from classes and extracurriculars. I had bought a ton of cheap liquor, thinking it would be enough for everyone.

Looking back, it was a terrible decision leading to a night of regret.

As the party went on, people started getting drunk, and things got out of hand. I remember having a drunk pillow fight with some of my friends, and things started getting blurry. The next thing I knew, everyone was throwing up, and my apartment was full of vomit. It was unbearable because of the smell. It was a disgusting and embarrassing sight for all at the time, even though those who made it to graduation laugh about it now.

The next morning, I woke up with a massive hangover in the back of my car trunk. I didn't remember much from the night before. As I cleaned up the mess, the reality of what happened started sinking in. I made a huge mistake by not being more responsible and thinking about the consequences of my actions.

I realized that I had put myself and my friends in danger by providing too much alcohol and not having a plan for the party. I also put my reputation and living situation at risk by letting things get out of hand. It was a humbling experience that made me reconsider my priorities and actions.

The consequences of my actions were severe. I had to clean up the mess and deal with the damage to my apartment. Some of my friends were mad at me for getting them too drunk, and I had to work to repair those relationships. I also realized that my reputation as a responsible and trustworthy person had been damaged.

Through this experience, I learned the importance of being responsible and thinking about the consequences of my actions.

Getting caught up in the excitement of throwing a party and drinking with friends is easy, but it's important to do so responsibly and safely. Looking back, I realize I should have planned the party more carefully and set clear boundaries for alcohol consumption.

The night I threw a party that ended in disaster was a wakeup call for me. It taught me the importance of being responsible and thinking about the consequences of my actions. Waking up in the trunk of my car with the trunk shut was a scary and humbling experience that made me reconsider my priorities and actions. I hope that by sharing this story, others can learn from my mistakes and avoid making similar ones.

Chapter 7: The Conversation About Bad Grades

As a college student, I experienced a situation that many students fear: talking to their parents about bad grades or retaking a course. It all started when I had difficulty adjusting to the demands of college life. I struggled with time management, procrastination, and a lack of study skills. As a result, I received low grades on my exams and assignments, which led to a disastrous first semester. By the end of the semester, my grades were so low that I had to have a difficult conversation with my parents about my academic standing.

During the conversation, I was overwhelmed with anxiety and anger. I felt ashamed, embarrassed, and disappointed in myself. My parents were also disappointed, and they made it clear that they would not pay for me to attend college if I didn't get my grades. In hindsight, I realized I could have avoided this situation if I had sought help earlier. I should have contacted my professors, academic advisors, and peers for support. Instead, I tried to handle everything independently, which only worsened things.

The aftermath of the conversation was tough. I had to pay for my tuition and find a way to improve my grades while balancing work and school. It was a challenging time, but it taught me valuable lessons about responsibility, self-discipline, and the importance of seeking help when needed.

Through this experience, I learned that it is okay to ask for help when you need it. College can be overwhelming, and getting lost in the demands of coursework and extracurricular activities is easy. Seeking support from professors, advisors, tutors, and peers can make all the difference in your academic success.

If you find yourself in a similar situation, don't be afraid to talk to your parents or guardians. Be honest about your struggles and explain what you're doing to improve your grades. Take responsibility for your actions and show you're committed to making changes.

The conversation I dreaded about my bad grades was a wakeup call for me. It taught me the importance of seeking help and taking responsibility for my actions. I hope that by sharing this story, I can encourage other students to seek support and avoid making similar mistakes. Remember that your college years are a time to learn and grow, including making mistakes. How you learn from those mistakes will define your success in college and beyond.

Chapter 8: The Road Trip That Went Wrong

One day, my friends and I decided to take a spontaneous road trip to the Florida Keys. We piled into my friend's old, beat-up car and set off on what we thought would be a fun adventure.

As we got further away from campus, we realized we hadn't planned the trip. We had no maps or GPS and decided to take the non-toll back roads to save money. This was a big mistake because we quickly lost cell service.

After a few hours of driving, the car suddenly broke down on the side of the road. We were in the middle of nowhere, no idea where the nearest gas station was. We had no choice but to push the car two miles to the nearest gas station, where we hoped we could find help.

The experience was both scary and hilarious at the same time. We were all pushing the car and laughing at how ridiculous the situation was. We were also anxious about being stranded in the middle of nowhere with no way to contact anyone for help.

Looking back, I realized that we should have planned the trip better. We should have brought maps, ensured the car was in good condition, and had a backup plan in case something went wrong. We also should have taken the toll roads to avoid losing cell service.

The consequences of our poor planning were having to push the car, being stranded in the middle of nowhere, and a stressful start to what was supposed to be a fun trip. But the positive consequences were that we learned a valuable lesson about the importance of planning and being prepared.

I learned from this experience to always plan ahead, even for the most spontaneous trips. Bring maps, make sure your car is in good condition, and have a backup plan in emergencies. This experience also taught me to find humor in stressful situations and to make the best of unexpected challenges.

The road trip to the Florida Keys was a memorable experience that taught me valuable lessons about planning, preparation, and making the best of unexpected challenges. I hope that by sharing this story, I can encourage others to be better prepared for spontaneous adventures and find humor in challenging situations.

Chapter 9: How My First College Relationship Almost Ruined My Academic Career

During my first semester of college, I got into a relationship with a girl I met at a party. It was exciting, and I wanted to spend all my time with her. As a result, I started skipping classes and neglecting my schoolwork. I even spent large amounts of money on her; I bought her expensive gifts and treated her to lavish dinners. I was so infatuated with her that I didn't realize my so-called relationship's impact on my grades and future.

At first, I didn't think anything of it. I was happy and in love, and that was all that mattered. But as the weeks went on, I started to notice that my grades were slipping. I was barely attending classes, and when I did, I was too distracted to focus. I spent all my time with my significant other and neglected my studies. It wasn't until I received my college's Satisfactory Academic Progress (SAP) warning that I realized how serious the situation had become.

I was scared and anxious about my academic standing. I had never been in this situation before and didn't know what to do. I was also angry at myself for letting my relationship get in the way of my studies. I felt like I had let myself down, and I was disappointed that I had risked my future for someone who didn't have my best interests at heart.

Looking back, I realize I should have set boundaries and prioritized my studies over my relationship. I should have communicated with my partner about the importance of my education and the impact their actions were having on my grades. I also should have sought help from my professors and academic advisors before it was too late.

The aftermath of the experience was devastating. I had to face the consequences of my actions and try to improve my grades while dealing with the emotional fallout of the relationship. I had to make up for missed assignments and attend extra tutoring sessions. I also had to have a difficult conversation with my partner and end the relationship, which was painful but necessary.

This experience taught me the importance of setting boundaries and prioritizing my studies. I learned that relationships are important but should never come at the expense of your education or future. I also learned the importance of seeking help and communicating with others when needed.

If you are in a similar situation, taking a step back and evaluating your priorities is important. Make sure to communicate with your partner about the importance of your education and set boundaries that work for both of you. Don't be afraid to seek help from your professors or academic advisors if you're struggling in class. Remember, your education is the foundation for your future, and it's important to prioritize it above all else.

Through this experience, I learned that it's important to prioritize your responsibilities and set boundaries in your relationships. College is a time for exploration and growth, but it's also a time for academic achievement. It's important to find a balance between your personal life and your academic goals.

If you are in a similar situation, don't be afraid to seek help. Talk to your academic advisor or a counselor about your struggles. They can provide you with resources and support to help you get back on track.

The relationship I entered into during my first semester of college was a learning experience for me. It taught me the importance of setting boundaries and prioritizing my responsibilities. I hope that by sharing this story, I can help other students avoid making similar mistakes and achieve their academic goals.

Chapter 10: Home Sick and Alone

During my first and second years of college, I experienced a situation that many college students can relate to being homesick. It all started when I moved away from my family to attend college in a new city, 16 hours from home. I was excited about the new adventure but realized how much I would miss home.

During those times, I was home sick for three weeks each year. I remember feeling deeply sad and longing for my family and familiar surroundings. I cried at night and struggled to get out of bed in the morning. I often skipped class or social events because I shook the feelings of loneliness and isolation.

I felt lost, alone, and like I had made a terrible mistake by moving away from home. I missed the comfort of my bed, the smell of my mom's cooking, and the sound of my siblings' laughter. I was homesick to the point of physical pain.

Looking back, I realized that I could have handled the situation differently. Instead of isolating myself, I should have contacted friends, family, or a counselor for support. I also could have made more of an effort to explore my new surroundings and create a sense of home away from home.

One consequence of being homesick was that I missed out on important experiences and opportunities. I regret not fully participating in social events or academic opportunities during that time. Another consequence was its impact on my mental health, which affected my emotional well-being.

This experience taught me the importance of seeking support when feeling overwhelmed or homesick. Creating a sense of home and belonging by connecting with others or finding comfort in familiar activities is also important. Additionally, I learned that taking a break and prioritizing my well-being is okay.

Being home sick was a challenging experience, but it taught me valuable lessons about the importance of seeking support and creating a sense of home away from home. I hope to help others experiencing similar loneliness and isolation by sharing this story.

Chapter 11: Surviving My First Serious Illness Without My Parents

I experienced a significant health setback during my first year at college. I was diagnosed with both pneumonia and the flu, and this was the first time I had ever gotten seriously ill away from home. The experience was physically and emotionally challenging, and I had to navigate the healthcare system independently.

Before getting sick, I had been feeling run down for a few days but attributed it to the stress of college life. However, my condition worsened, and I began to experience severe coughing, fever, and fatigue.

I knew I needed medical attention but could not drive to the hospital. I tried calling an Uber, but none of the drivers wanted to take me because I was coughing and had a fever. I was terrified, and I didn't know what to do.

Finally, I called my mom, who lived sixteen hours away and asked her to call an Uber for me. I was terribly sick and had no other choice but to call my mother and ask her to call me an Uber. It was embarrassing!

The Uber driver was kind enough to take me to the hospital, where I was diagnosed with pneumonia and the flu. I was given antibiotics and sent home to recover.

I was scared, alone, and completely out of my depth. I felt like a child again, unable to care for myself or manage my own healthcare. It was a humbling experience, and I had to confront the reality that I was no longer a child and needed to learn to take care of myself.

Looking back on the experience, I realize I should have sought medical attention earlier. I also should have had a plan for situations like this, such as a local urgent care clinic or a trusted doctor to call.

The experience had both positive and negative consequences. On the one hand, I learned to be more independent and take responsibility for my healthcare. On the other hand, I struggled with anxiety and worried about my health, and the experience made me feel more homesick and isolated.

The moral of the story was that I learned the importance of having a support system and a plan for healthcare emergencies. I also learned that it's okay to ask for help when needed and that being vulnerable can sometimes lead to better outcomes.

If you're living away from home for the first time, having a plan for healthcare emergencies is important. This might include finding a local urgent care clinic or doctor, having a trusted friend or family member to call in case of an emergency, and keeping important medical information on hand. It's also important to listen to your body and seek medical attention early if you suspect you might be getting sick. Finally, don't be afraid to ask for help or reach out to your support system when you need it.

Chapter 12: The Truth About Financial Aid

Entering college financial aid was the first thing on my mind; I worried about costs and needing a job. The university I went to said there was a set price for students that is only based on the year you entered; they did not stick by this statement raising the price every year.

As a second-generation college student, I knew that financial aid would be essential in helping me afford the cost of tuition. When I received my financial aid award letter, I was relieved to see that I would receive enough aid to cover the full cost of tuition and some of my living expenses. I thought the amount of financial aid listed on my award letter was set in stone and that I did not have to worry about any surprise expenses. However, as I entered my second year of college, I was shocked to receive a bill from the university stating that my tuition had increased by thousands of dollars. Confused and frustrated, I contacted the financial aid office, and they told me that the amount of financial aid I received was only based on the previous year's cost of attendance and did not include any increases for the upcoming year. I was disappointed and deceived by the university, which had promised a set price for students based on their year of entry.

I had to take out multiple loans to cover the increased tuition and living expenses. When I asked the financial aid office why they had not honored their original statement, they denied ever making such a claim. I learned that I should have gotten their promise in writing, as I had no proof of the initial agreement. I felt angry and cheated, paying so much more than I had planned. I was also worried about how I could pay off the additional loans and how it would affect my financial situation after graduation.

Looking back, I realize I should have researched and asked more questions before accepting my financial aid award. I also learned that getting any promises or agreements in writing is essential to protect myself in case of unexpected changes.

The aftermath of the experience was difficult. I had to work extra hours at my job and take out additional loans to cover the increased cost of tuition. It took me longer to pay off my student loans, affecting my financial situation after graduation.

The key lesson I learned from this experience is the importance of thoroughly researching and asking questions to understand the terms of financial aid fully. I also learned the importance of getting any written agreements or promises to protect myself from unexpected changes. It is important to be proactive and take control of my financial situation to avoid any surprises that could affect my future.

Chapter 13: Navigating Professor Problems

Entering college, I was excited to pursue a degree in a field I was passionate about. I enrolled in the major program I had been dreaming of and was eager to learn and grow under the guidance of my professors. However, I quickly realized that not all professors were supportive and encouraging.

Explain what led up to the experience: I had always been interested in pursuing a career in a specific field, and my major program aligned perfectly with my goals. I was determined to succeed and put in much hard work and dedication. However, I noticed that one particular professor, the head of the major program, seemed distant and uninterested in me.

Despite my efforts to engage with the professor, I always felt a sense of disinterest from him. He would make offhand comments that made me feel like I didn't belong and was not cut out for the field. Eventually, he told me outright that I did not fit the "stereotype" of someone pursuing the major and was not cut out for it.

I felt devastated by the professor's comments. I had worked hard to pursue my dreams, and his lack of support and encouragement was demotivating. I started to doubt myself and my abilities, wondering if I was not cut out for the field.

Looking back, I realize that I should have taken action earlier. I should have spoken up and asked for help from other professors or academic advisors. Instead, I let the negative comments fester, affecting my motivation and self-esteem.

The experience with the professor made me feel discouraged and disheartened. I lost my passion for the field and ultimately had to change my major and career path. The negative comments affected me deeply and affected my confidence and self-belief.

The consequences of the experience were significant. Changing my major and career path did not delay my graduation but resulted in additional stress and financial burden, and medical school was no longer an option.

I learned that not all professors would be supportive and encouraging, but seeking resources and support from others is important. Academic advisors, peers, and other professors can offer guidance and help navigate difficult situations. Additionally, it's important not to let negative comments from one individual affect your motivation and self-esteem.

If you find yourself in a similar situation, seek support from other resources. Don't let one negative experience define your entire academic or career path. Remember that you are capable and deserving of success; seek mentors who will support and encourage you.

Chapter 14: Winning at All Costs

Throughout my college years, I enjoyed participating in recreational sports on campus, including soccer, basketball, football, volleyball, and kickball. However, each season in the playoffs, there would always be an altercation fueled by leftover high school testosterone.

During the football season, my team and I made it to the championship game, and we were playing against a team that was getting beat 72 to 7. The opposing team was upset, and tensions were high. As the game ended, one of their players made a dirty hit on me, and a scuffle broke out. It quickly escalated into a full-blown fight, with players from both teams throwing punches and tackling each other.

During the altercation, I felt a mix of anger and adrenaline. It was frustrating to see that winning had become more important than sportsmanship. I was also concerned for the safety of myself and my teammates.

Looking back on the experience, I realized that the competitive atmosphere had taken away from the enjoyment of playing recreational sports. Seeing how quickly things could turn violent when winning was the sole focus was disheartening. In the future, I knew I needed to be more mindful of my behavior and prioritize sportsmanship over winning.

The aftermath of the altercation was not pleasant. The opposing team was disqualified from the league and suspended many players. It also left a sour taste in my mouth about participating in recreational sports on campus.

Through this experience, I learned that winning should never come at the cost of good sportsmanship and the safety of others. It's important to enjoy the game and not let the competitive atmosphere take over. Additionally, I realized that I needed to be mindful of my behavior and positively influence my team.

If you find yourself in a similar situation, it's important to remember that sportsmanship should always come first. Don't let the competitive atmosphere cloud your judgment, and always prioritize the safety of yourself and others. Recreational sports should be enjoyable, and winning should not be the only goal.

35

Chapter 15: The Cost of Indulgence

My second year at college was amazing because I learned a lot. During my first year of college, I discovered a new restaurant near campus that quickly became my weakness. Whenever I was hungry, I would go there and eat as if it were my last meal. The food was delicious, the atmosphere was cozy, and the staff was friendly. Before I knew it, I ate there almost every day, and the costs quickly increased.

Over the course of the second semester, I ended up spending roughly $2,500 on eating out at that same restaurant. I had become so addicted to the food that I didn't even realize how much I was spending until I received my credit card statement. But the cost was not the only consequence of my eating habits.

I also gained approximately 50 pounds throughout the semester without realizing it. My clothes no longer fit, and I struggled to keep up with the demands of my classes. My grades began to suffer, and I felt more tired and sluggish than ever before.

It was hard to accept that I had indulged in unhealthy foods and overspending dining out. I was back to square one when I blew $3000 on the vending machine. I had prioritized my cravings over my health and my financial stability. I knew I needed to make a change.

At first, I was not aware where to start. The more I thought about my spending habits, the clearer it became. I knew where to start and recognized that I needed to do something. I started by setting a budget for eating out and limiting myself to once a week. I also began to meal prep and cook healthier meals at home. It was a challenge at first, but I soon found that I enjoyed the process of cooking and planning my meals. With the support of my friends and family, I was able to lose the weight I had gained and improve my academic performance.

Looking back, I realized that my experience was not just about food and money but about self-discipline and making choices that align with my goals and values. It is easy to get caught up in the excitement of trying new restaurants and indulging in our cravings, but keeping our health and financial goals in mind is important.

My experience taught me a valuable lesson about the consequences of overspending on dining out and indulging in unhealthy foods. By reflecting on my habits and making positive changes, I was able to turn things around and achieve my goals. I hope that by sharing this story, I can inspire others to make healthy choices and take control of their finances.

Chapter 16: Hacked: My Credit Card Nightmare

As a college sophomore, I had been using my credit card responsibly for months. I had never missed a payment and felt confident in managing my finances. However, one day, I received an alert that my credit card had been charged $645 at a Sun Glass Hut. I immediately knew something was wrong.

Before the incident, I had used my credit card for various purchases, including textbooks, groceries, and occasional dining out. I always checked my balance and never exceeded my credit limit.

After receiving the alert about the unauthorized charge, I immediately contacted my credit card company and reported the fraud. I had to cancel my credit card and order a new one. It was time-consuming, and I had to wait several days to receive the new card.

The fraud occurred at a Sun Glass Hut, but I didn't know who was involved. It was likely that someone had obtained my credit card information illegally.

I felt violated and frustrated. I believe someone had stolen my credit card information and used it without my consent. I also felt vulnerable and worried about the potential consequences of the fraud.

I realized I had become complacent about monitoring my credit card transactions. I should have been more vigilant and checked my account more frequently.

Discuss the impact of the experience on the author: The fraud caused me stress and inconvenience, as I had to cancel my credit card and wait for a new one. It also made me question my ability to manage my finances and made me feel vulnerable.

The fraud harmed my credit score, as it was a disputed charge on my credit report. It also caused me to be more cautious about using my credit card and to monitor my transactions more closely.

The experience taught me the importance of monitoring my credit card transactions and being more proactive about protecting my personal information. It also made me realize that credit card fraud can happen to anyone, no matter how responsible they are with their finances.

Regularly check credit card transactions, monitor credit reports, and report any unauthorized charges immediately to the credit card company.

Use caution when providing credit card information online, regularly monitor credit card transactions, and take steps to protect personal information, such as using secure passwords and avoiding sharing personal information with unknown parties.

Chapter 17: Beware of the Forbidden Topics

In college, I met friends I thought would be lifelong companions. We bonded over our shared interests and experiences, but our differences began to surface as time passed.

We all came from different backgrounds and held different beliefs about religion, race, and politics. At first, our conversations were respectful and engaging, but our disagreements became more heated as tensions grew in the world around us.

Arguments broke out over social media, at parties, and even in our dorm rooms. People took sides, and friendships were strained. Eventually, the group disbanded entirely, with no one speaking to each other anymore.

The events took place on and off campus, involving about 10 people. The arguments involved personal attacks and hurtful words, leading to the disintegration of the entire friend group.

I was devastated to lose friends I had grown close to over the years. I was also frustrated with the lack of understanding and respect that some of my former friends showed toward others.

Looking back, I realize that we could have handled our disagreements better. We should have focused on finding common ground and respecting each difference.

The experience made me more aware of the importance of respectful communication and understanding. It also made me appreciate the friends that I have now who share my values and beliefs.

The consequences of the disintegration of the friend group were negative, as we all lost important relationships. However, it also taught us all valuable lessons about communication, empathy, and respect.

The experience taught me to be more intentional with my friendships and to prioritize respectful communication and understanding.

Important to find common ground and respect each difference, especially regarding sensitive topics like religion, race, and politics. We should prioritize respectful communication and understanding in our relationships.

Practice active listening, understand others' perspectives, and prioritize respectful communication in your relationships.

Chapter 18: Lessons Learned: Reflections on a College Journey

As the story of my college years ends, I can't help but reflect on the numerous mishaps, mistakes, and challenges I encountered along the way. From spending thousands of dollars on vending machines to tearing my labrum while playing basketball, my experiences have taught me valuable lessons that I hope will benefit others.

While some of my stories may seem like cautionary tales, I think they are opportunities for growth and learning. Brushing $3,000 on vending machines may not have been my finest moment, but it taught me the value of financial responsibility and the dangers of impulse spending.

In retrospect, I can now laugh at the time I had to retake a class six times because I didn't follow the rubric. It was frustrating at the time, but it taught me the importance of paying attention to details and following instructions.

And who can forget the road trip that went wrong? Pushing a car two miles to the nearest gas station wasn't the most enjoyable experience, but it gave me a newfound appreciation for the kindness of strangers.

Of course, not all of my experiences were lighthearted. Navigating serious illnesses without my parents and struggling with homesickness were some of the most difficult times in my life. But they also taught me resilience and the importance of seeking support from friends and professionals.

As I wrap up my college journey, I'm reminded of the importance of learning from our mistakes and taking them in stride. College may have been filled with ups and downs, but it was also a time of growth, exploration, and discovery.

And for those about to embark on college journeys, don't worry - you're not alone. I'm compiling a book of roommate horror stories from college. Stay tuned for "College Chronicles: Roommate Edition," coming soon.

I hope that my experiences and reflections can serve as a helpful guide for others navigating the ups and downs of college life. Remember to take risks, learn from your mistakes, and don't forget to have a sense of humor along the way. Cheers to the next chapter!

Despite all these challenges, I was determined to finish what I had started. It was not always easy, and there were times when I wanted to give up. But I knew that giving up was not an option. I persevered through the late nights, the failed classes, the personal struggles, and the financial difficulties.

Graduating with a 3.4 GPA and a bachelor's degree on time was a huge accomplishment for me, and it showed me that I could overcome obstacles and achieve my goals. And now, pursuing a master's degree is a testament to my determination and hard work.

Perseverance is not just about overcoming obstacles, it's also about the attitude and mindset you have when facing them. It's about not giving up, even when things get tough. It's about having the courage to keep going, even when you don't know the outcome.

One thing I've learned from my college experience is that perseverance is key to success. No matter what challenges you face, you can overcome them with the right mindset and attitude. And even if you stumble along the way, you can still pick yourself up and keep moving forward.

So, to all the college students, remember that it's okay to fail, make mistakes, and struggle. But what's not okay is to give up. Persevere through the tough times, and you'll become stronger on the other side. The college journey may be challenging, but it is also rewarding, and with perseverance, you can achieve anything you set your mind to.

Synopsis

The Unofficial Guide to Surviving College is a collection of stories reflecting the defining moments of the author's life. Through 18 chapters, the author shares personal experiences and valuable lessons learned during their college journey. From the consequences of indulgence to the importance of following a rubric, each story is unique in its own way, but they are all connected by a common thread: the power of learning from our mistakes. The author hopes that by sharing their own experiences, they can inspire others to reflect on their own and learn from their mistakes. This book is dedicated to all the individuals who have played a role in the author's personal and professional development.

Upcoming Publications

1. Book 2: Roommate Horror Stories (Early Summer 2023)
2. Book 3: "Avoiding the 'F' Word: A Guide to Passing Your Classes" - A witty handbook on how to study and succeed in college classes. (Early Summer 2023)
3. Book 4: "Living on a Budget: How to Stretch Your Ramen Noodle Fund" - A laugh-out-loud guide to making your college budget last. (Early Fall 2023)
4. Book 5: "From Frat Parties to the Library: Finding Your Balance" - A fun guide to balancing your social life and academic responsibilities. (Late Fall 2023)
5. Book 6: "The College Dating Handbook: How to Swipe Left on Disappointment" - A lighthearted look at navigating the dating scene in college. (Early Winter 2023)
6. Book 7: Adulting 101: Graduating and Transitioning to the Real World (Without Crying). (Late Winter 2023)